BUTCH
GEOGRAPHY

BUTCH

GEOGRAPHY

Poems

STACEY WAITE

TUPELO PRESS

North Adams, Massachusetts

Library of Congress Cataloging-in-Publication Data
Waite, Stacey.
 [Poems. Selections]
 Butch Geography : poems / Stacey Waite. -- First edition.
      pages   cm
 ISBN 978-1-936797-25-7 (paperback original)
 I. Title.
 PS3623.A356558B88 2013
 811'.6–dc23
                        2012045095

Cover and text designed by Howard Klein.
Cover art: "Handle" by Don Ross (http://donrossphotography.com).
Used with permission of the artist.

First edition: January 2013.

Tupelo Press
P.O. Box 1767
243 Union Street, Eclipse Mill, Loft 305
North Adams, Massachusetts 01247
Telephone: (413) 664–9611 / Fax: (413) 664–9711
editor@tupelopress.org / www.tupelopress.org

Tupelo Press is an award-winning independent literary press that publishes fine fiction, nonfiction, and poetry in books that are a joy to hold as well as read. Tupelo Press is a registered 501(c)3 non-profit organization, and we rely on public support to carry out our mission of publishing extraordinary work that may be outside the realm of large commercial publishers. Financial donations are welcome and are tax deductible.

For Brie

Contents

I

II

III

IV

I

I do not come to you
save that I confess to being
half man and half
woman. I have seen the ivy cling
to a piece of crumbled
wall so that you cannot tell
by which either
stands: this is to say
if she to whom I cling
is loosened both
of us go down.

William Carlos Williams

On the Occasion of Being Mistaken for a Boy by the Umpire
in the Little League Conference Championship

I had learned quickly how to spit
through the jail-like bars of the catcher's mask
so looking back I can't say as I blame the umpire
who, after seeing me spit and punch my glove,
could only draw one conclusion:
"You got your cup on, right son?"

And almost everyone hears him, and I
want my father to stand up, like he does, and yell,
"What the hell are you looking at, bub!"
or "Bad call, blue!" But instead there's a hush,
and I forget the signs for curve balls, fast balls,
and screw balls, and all I can think about is no balls,

no little ten-year-old balls to match my spit
and mitt-punching. My mother pretends
to clean up orange peels and the boys yell
from the infield, "It's a girl, we got a girl as catcher."
He doesn't know what to say so follows up "Alrighty"
with a quick "Play ball." But I can't squat now,

I think everyone is looking at my no balls.
They're all watching the girl with no balls.
I'm watching her, too. She knows better
than to cry so spits again. She learns
to live in halves, to, as her father says,
"Save it for the field." She snaps,
"What are you blind, Ump?" and digs
her plastic spikes into the fresh dirt.

Self-Portrait, 1984

Dad tells Mom I'll end up a dyke
from playing ice hockey.
And my brother tells me a dyke
is a girl who likes other girls.
And I don't like girls at all—
they only play jump rope at recess.
And Jackie Wellman smells
like fruit every single day.

Sometimes no one can keep my mom
from crying. I think the frying pans
get grease in her eyes when she cooks,
so I always say I don't like anything hot.
It's okay to lie about food, I think.

When I take my bike on the horse trails,
there are towers that make sounds
like a baby singing, but the babies
are invisible. My dad says no one
is invisible but God. Sometimes
I pretend the barn is my house.
Sometimes I take my bike apart
and put it back together all morning.

No one knows what I can do.
If you won't tell, I'll jump no hands
from the hayloft door.
I made a house out of boxes
in the woods. I could live there
if I wanted, if I wasn't scared
of the tree limbs snatching me up.
My dad says trees are alive.
And I think they just might
do something bad if they could.

Letter to Brian Nelson, Who Chanted *Boy or a Girl, Boy or a Girl* at Me on the Playground During Recess

Maybe your father wasn't much of a listener.
Maybe you're worried I'll never give up this tire swing,
and it'll leave you with some kind of tire-swing blue balls
while I'm spinning on this black rubber ring refusing
to surrender to your playground intimidation tactics,
your leaning at the wood post, your gender song.

Brian Nelson, maybe I should say I'm sorry
my biceps are bigger and rounder than yours,
sorry my voice falls deep five years before yours,
sorry my brother's Wranglers make me
the coolest of cowboys scaling the metal rails
of the monkey bars, sorry, too, that I hit home runs
over your head in Mrs. Garafalo's gym class.

      Boy or a girl?
      Boy or a girl?

Brian Nelson, I will not leave this tire swing.
I will not put down this GI Joe. I will not stop
kissing your sister in the sandbox. I will not stop
spitting in the woods. Brian Nelson, your hands are
little machetes, your voice a small army of soldiers.
Brian Nelson, did you know that female hyenas
mount the males? Did you know you cannot tell
the gender of a loon without cutting it open?
Did you know some cultures worship androgyny?
They call us all-knowers. And I know you,
Brian Nelson. I know how hard it is
to be a boy. I know how hard it is
to protect masculinity, its skin as thin
and fragile as the holy playground air.

In Second Grade Robby O'Reilly Punches Me in the Eye Because I Lost the Garter Snake I Was Supposed to Watch While He Went Camping with His Father in Maine

Put the lid on tight, he says.
The snake is yellow
yellow like a bee's body
yellow like a dandelion
yellow like a summer's day
yellow like the belly of a yellow fish
its body thick and long
its face rough like a fire-sung rock song.

The snake escaped, I don't know how, I say.
Loser, he says and punches.
As I lie in the grass pulling back tears
as I watch the sky above me spin like a blue-white top
I imagine the snake turning into a river, its body
exploding into water, its skin clear liquid
encircling the rocks, its tail water winding
through the trees, emptying out
into an ocean, black and blue.

Boys in Trees

I remember her leaning at the sink,
always the gray wet line on her shirt.
My mother's cooking begins with peeling:
the dirt skin of potato, the pulling of thick
orange strands, opaque flakes of carrot.

After peeling, she cannot bear the boiling
and softening, the smell of the meats
dropped in the pan. It all seems to be dying.
Or maybe she knows her children cannot
help but ingest some element of death.

In summer, she pushes hard on the lemons
until they bleed clear. Sometimes,
from up in the red oak beside the house,
we hear her crying. We are boys in trees.
My brother shifts and sighs, *we don't*
even need that lemon water. We wait
up in the tree for her to call us. We wait
until the lemon rind has been tossed out
in the side yard. We drink it then, when
there is nothing left of what our mother
had never, not even once, wanted.

The Monkeys

Consider the monkeys who live most of their lives
in trees, running across the branches.
Like us, they smile and yawn, which turns out later
to signal attack. They piss on each other as a sign
of dominance. They groom one another to mean
I love you, I'm sorry we fought, or *We are a troop.*
For a monkey, staring is a threat, eye contact
a time bomb of bite and scratch.

Consider that I refused my mother's grooming
all my life: *no you cannot paint my nails, no*
you cannot braid my hair, no I will not sit
while you comb out the knots, no I will not sit
still while you wipe my face with a warm cloth.

In the end it's my voice that makes people stare.
Humans stare at one another to mean *What are you?*
the time bomb of bite and scratch.

Consider that monkeys have thirty kinds of vocalization.
One to mean *Stay out.* One to mean *Mine.* One
to mean *Excuse me,* and *Wait,* and *Yes.*

Consider the night my grandfather died.
He stared at me for hours under fluorescent light,
the blank stare of too many hospital machines,
time bomb of bite and scratch.

Perhaps if all the staring stopped. Perhaps if
smiles and yawns would never turn on us.
Perhaps then, grieving mother, you might
bring in the warm cloth, and touch it
to my irreverent and impossible face.

Self-Portrait, 1986

I like to take my shirt off outside, I like lying
bare skin, my back to the cooled wet blacktop
where my father has washed his vintage Chevy,
the soap suds tingling my shoulder blades.
I don't like the fourth grade one bit.
I don't like my brothers, how they get to be boys,
how they're allowed to jump from the hayloft door.
I don't like when people say "little girl," or when
we have to change in the locker room and get ready
for girls' gym class, which is different from boys'
gym class. I don't like watching the boys play
crab soccer through the window. I don't like
disco aerobics while I'm watching the boys
hold up their bodies on their hands. This church
dress won't last. Tell you what I'm gonna do:
I'm gonna ride my bike to the horse trails.
I'm gonna bury the dress out by the horse farm.
I'm gonna bury it so deep, the dogs can't even
dig it up. Sometimes I can't keep promises.
Sometimes I pack my flashlight and cereal,
and I sneak out of the house at night. I have
every intention of living in the woods. I breathe
in the dark air. I pretend everyone is listening
to what I want to say. I sing the Pet Shop Boys
under the sycamore. Sometimes the world
is too small for a kid like me. The Pet Shop Boys
are from England. England is far, so far
that if I could get to it, no one, not one single
person, could find me. Not anyone. Not ever.

Elegy

It's usually pigeons that gather
at the park bench to lift and drop the bread
we couldn't hold on to.
But today, it's the crows dipping their short black beaks
into the body of a dead sparrow.

"Shame on them," my father says, "picking at their own kind."
My father will die ten years from this park bench.
When I kneel before his body at the Catholic mass,
I will gather my fingers together.
I will appear to be praying.

The sparrow's body leaves a brown stain on the sidewalk
when the crows finally drag him to the grass.

Ten years from this park bench, my brothers
will carry my father's body to be buried.
I will walk behind them, hands empty,
no memory of having ever prayed at all.

Kimberly

Kimberly is the girl who played hopscotch on the blacktop.
I threw crickets at Kimberly on field trips.
Kimberly wouldn't have been caught with her shirt off
at the public pool, wouldn't have shaved her face
in the third grade, or called them "bad ass poppa wheelies."
My mother wanted to name me Kimberly.

I might have made better decisions about my hair
or done more sit-ups. I might have waited
to have sex with a man, thought it something special.
I might have drawn something more appropriate
for the refrigerator door. I might have practiced
spelling my name over and over in cursive.
Kimberly, I should have been Kimberly.
I would have felt some loyalty to a name like that.

It Has Always Been Frankie Cossinelli

Ever since his baseball jacket that fit me
like pantyhose for the upper body,
which could make me into a kind of masked thief
if you think about it, and I could run around
robbing gas stations in my Frankie Cossinelli mask,
which is really a jacket but fits like a mask.
And then he dumps me and my mother says,
"There are other fish in the sea,"
when really she means, "You will spend years
trying to drown yourself, just like I do,
over men you have never loved," except for this moment
when you put his tiny man jacket on your big woman belly
and your friends say, "Frankie likes you,"
which means the world is your oyster,
but then you remember you hate oysters and pearls
and there must be something else to find in this sea,
like Frankie Cossinelli's cousin Anthony,
who is allergic to beestings and wears the same Metallica T-shirt
every day because his parents are never home
when he leaves for school in the dark quiet mornings,
where being thirteen is enough sin for all of us.
The thing is, I didn't love Frankie or Anthony.
They were ways of defining the self with baseball jackets
and shiny gold nameplates on hickeyed-up necks
that meant I belonged to someone and therefore
was not responsible for my actions, which a good
fraction of the time were not nice. I was a not nice teenager,
the kind of girl who'd "call you out"
in the courtyard if you looked at her wrong,
the kind of girl who wore stretch jeans and black concert T-shirts
so you'd know she was a piece of night sky,
the kind of girl who didn't blow her runny nose,
but just sniffed all day long. Other girls
wanted to be me, to have that night sky power,

but I was Frankie Cossinelli's girl.
And the day he left me for Jennifer Seaman
(funny in both the sperm sense and
the sailor-at-sea sense) I locked myself
in the bathroom and cried tears
that from this night sky body were really stars.

Tits

First day of school. Seventh grade.
Jackie Bachman says, "Hey,
you got your tits this summer!"
And I roll my shoulders forward,
the huge wrecking balls of that summer
pressing their flesh on my hanging belly.

"Shut up, bitch," I say,
speaking the language of girls,
girls with white Candies sneakers,
girls with high hair,
girls with blue abyss eye shadow,
girls who wished for
perfect, perky and bouncing tits.

Jackie saunters off, and when she is out of sight,
I run—past the Dugard's choo-choo train mailbox,
over Mr. Sandler's green, no-trespassing suburban lawn,
through my father's piles of raked leaves and twigs.
Frantic and panting, I reach the door
to find my mother at the glass, Windex in hand,
singing the wrong words to another Billy Joel song.

And suddenly I hate her,
with her blue sweatpants and her Giants T-shirt,
inspecting the glass like a complicated plot.
I wish my breath would turn into a black smut
and take over the narrative of her window.
I want to stop the washing.
I want to dirty every little thing.
Whatcha runnin' from, sweets?

And I can't say I'm running from my tits,
I can't tell her Jackie Bachman is a bitch

and I don't want to wear any bras.
I can't tell her how I ran home carrying
these ugly mounds of fat flesh
and how with each quick step
I imagine a new and pulsing vein
branching straight out from my heart
to these darkening nipples.
Everyone will see them through my shirt.
Your turn to wash dishes, she says.
And I stand scrubbing pans, the flesh shaking
with each stroke, my body alive
and inevitable.

On the Occasion of Being Mistaken for the Delivery Boy by Two Members of the Girls Youth Soccer League at the Marriot Hotel

I am at the door, pizza in hand
like Galileo with the globe.
I can hear them giggling
from behind the door, their footsteps
pitter-pattering. It is probably
their first time ordering pizza alone.
Tipping the driver will be
a sweet new power for them.

I feel the eye pressed against
the proverbial peephole.
"Pizza guy's here," she says.
"And he is so cute."
I pull my red Mama Angelina's
hat over my eyes, which are
far too feminine and blue,
and when the door swings open,
I am at the gate of a new heaven:

I am the cute delivery boy who,
after he is spotted by neighborhood fathers,
is kept away from daughters such as these.
They want me to join them,
to pull up a badly upholstered chair
and share the pepperoni pie radiating wet
heat through its bottom like an engine.

I stay for a glorious hour,
tell stories about the band
I never played in, tell them
the guitar has just always come
natural to me—I am self-taught, I say.
I can play anything you want to hear by ear.

Shauna is the one of them I love,
her calves carved out like crescent moons
as she props her Adidas sneakers atop
the television, which is blaring
Prince's greatest hits on MTV.

"Can you play guitar like him?" she asks.
And I think on the question of Prince,
his small erotic body, his long hair falling
around his shoulders like a black scarf.
I lie and say, "I think Prince is a sissy."

I never said I played this role well.
Truth is, I made a bad delivery boy
and felt shame fall over my body
when Shauna pressed her mouth
against my cheek and called me
"a hottie." And when she asked me
where the band was playing next,
I said Detroit. And when she asked me
where I was headed from the hotel,
I said back to work. The truth is,
I played classical guitar on Sundays
for my grandmother, who called me
her "little Czechoslovakian Princess."

The truth is, I couldn't go back to work.
Truth is, I couldn't go home again either.

About Ben

When I was fourteen, I had a girlfriend named Janie. She was from
Smithtown, three miles west of my own small town where I was a Z.
Cavaricci–wearing, suburban junior high-schooler who spent her Friday
nights at the Commack Roller Rink with teased hair and hot-pink skate
wheels. But not with Janie. To Janie, I was Ben . . . Axl Rose–looking,
piano-playing, poem-writing Ben with long brown hair and peach fuzz
above the lip. She loved me. She loved the way I sang "Stairway to
Heaven" on her answering machine and wore a bulky black leather
jacket. "I want to see you with your shirt off," she says. "You are
probably so defined," she says. And Janie doesn't know how she's on
to something, how definition rests itself tightly rolled in the socks I have
zipped into the crotch of my big brother's Wranglers. Janie says I have
a gentle kiss, says her brother will kick my ass if he finds out we are
"frenching."

I am afraid I had to leave her though, one Saturday evening outside
the Sports Plus Entertainment Hall. I had to leave her standing there
beneath the blinking green ticket sign. She was asking too many
questions and the little bullets beneath the ace bandage wrapped
around my chest were ready to fire forth and I knew it. "But we kissed,"
Janie says. I tell her I can't help it. My parents are making me move
to Manhasset, which is a good thirty minutes away. I ask her for the
photo her friend Emily took of me smoking at Caleb Smith Park. She
must have no evidence of Ben. I tell her I don't want the photo to be
painful for her. She refuses to give it over. I tell her I will call but I don't,
can't risk it. The phone is dangerous when my father picks it up while
I am talking to Janie. "Stacey, I need the phone," he might say. And
what would happen to me then, sitting in those Z. Cavariccis with that
hair and creating the life of Ben. Ben's father, after all, had died. His
mother was a waitress and his stepfather hit him. Ben had it hard. Ben
only had one other girlfriend before, named Lisa. She was short and
had braces but Ben didn't mind. Ben was sensitive, didn't care about
things like looks. Ben wrote long beautiful poems about not so beautiful
girls. Ben did have a cousin named Stacey. Ben tells Janie she might

see her sometime and she will know the girl is his cousin because they look exactly alike. Ben is meticulous, covers all the bases. And when he walks away from her that Saturday, he dies a little, even at fourteen. He dies because he has lost everything.

Gesture Toward Seeing It Coming

Next to the sandbox, my father washes our dog,
his hands scrubbing its ears, under the legs.
I don't look at the sandbox, afraid of the worms
whose bodies had burst under my plastic shovel
weeks earlier. I don't look at my father because

I'm mad at him and don't know he will die
years later, don't know there will be an open casket
with his body in it, and people will cry and touch
the shoulders of his best suit. I don't know
they will make him up all wrong, the glue too thick
between his lips. I don't know I will end up,
years later when they lower him into the ground,

thinking about the worms again, twisting their rubbery
bodies over his body, pushing into the fading glue,
until one finds itself trapped between his silent lips.

Remembering a Full Moon, Threaded

I was young the first time
a boy forced his tongue

into my mouth. My mouth
felt full and open for days.

I couldn't forget his mouth
or remember that I was young,

that I spent afternoons hanging
from the hayloft door, that I would
crush lemons for my mother's water.

Dear Gender

You aren't always pretty, pretty like a summer's day,
pretty like the red of Strawberry Shortcake's dress,

pretty like the toss of Jennifer Aniston's hair outside
the set of another romantic comedy, busting up myths

of messages made whole, baseball cap to the prom,
four-wheeling Sundays in the thick dirt, you say:

Lincoln logs, no. Tonka trucks, no. Emotions, no.
Gender, rise out, an exorcism, from our too-scared skin.

Let us make the sounds we were never meant to make.
Let us curse. Let us drive. Let us grill steak in the yard.

Here I am, gender. Tell me again the girl I should be,
please, just say it quietly, so no one will hear.

The reverse side also has a reverse side.

Japanese Proverb

Butch Geography

The desert is butch
        Robin Becker

It's true some places are butch—
some locations, no matter how solid,
a quicksand of subversion. Cathedrals,
the mouths of sailors, the shedding
of pine trees in the yard, butch.
Where phones are ringing, where
suspension bridges rise up, butch.
Train stations, orchids, oak wood,
butch. The river with unbearable
currents, butch. Fires clearing
out the mountains, butch—
the maps, the trails themselves,
butch. Entire cities: Pittsburgh,
Tulsa, Los Angeles, Lincoln,
also butch. Infrastructure,
circus tents. Any place there is
wind, any place there are
sandstorms. Deserts, yes.
Playgrounds, yes. Beach dunes,
under the backs of bike tires,
yes. Wherever there is
cavernous depth, wherever
there are tapped-out wallets,
or strapped-on sex,
or pat-down checks
from cops on chests.
Wherever there is grit
dressed up as a gentleman.
Wherever there are
ladders and lips,
or shutters and bricks,
or man-things to fix.

Wherever there is factory-
made bravado, or a purely
chivalrous motto.
Indeed, in the desert—
barren, hot, and silent—
lizards and ring-tailed cats,
no water, cold nights,
the possibility of snake bites,
and yet—survival, the anthem
of those places we've always been.

When the Dead Ask for Maps

This is where I live. My father's dead voice
wants me to say I am a woman, not
a soldier or another woman's glacier,
refusing to sink into skin-deep sea.

We feel what we feel, and in this place
even the floorboards urge. Our shadows
know our real histories, how our mouths
have been mistresses in some tender hour.

In the way he spreads out like new roots
in the earth, my father is saying
that there is no redemption,
that I am overgrown and frozen.

I am not hungry. My mouth is inadequate.
My father doesn't like my lover because she
makes me what I am—beloved. Because she
makes me amber taken from his fossil.

I can't help but say what he wants
so I return to the place where it's not me.
I move outside myself to watch a woman,
who resembles me, but whose hands are empty
of wanting. She does what she's asked to do.

She is not a woman I want to love,
but her whisper, *Yes, father, I am a woman,*
moves and assures him.

Wedding Photo, 1968

My parents kneeling below a crucifix.
The walls look terribly like dead grass.

The priest's arm is raised above their heads
with the holy water. Only my father is more heroic.

The altar is a three-quarter moon, two
solitudes are falling into each other,
one is a lake, the other—rain.

They have a new metaphor for loving.
My mother's eyes are two brown mirrors.

This moment is a screen behind which our family
moves like a body, like they are in charge
of definitions, like their stomachs are not already full.

Later in the day, my father will pose for more photos,
his bride surrounded by the largeness of her dress,
the bouquets of flowers, yellow and wet.

When the relatives leave, he will make love to his new wife.
She will become the story he loves best, the one
where his hands are wisdom, the wicks of candles.

I don't want to love this moment,
this moment in which I forget
the secret my father tells while he kneels:

that his strength is some sort of dust,
that we will grow out of the cathedral walls.

Dear Gender

The truth is I've loved you always.
Despite your refusal to play with me,
your stage-fright, stubbornness
and cruel pranks, you have always been
up in tree branches with me like a sibling.

But there were nights, however brief,
when you fell to pieces in my lap,
tired hands covering your eyes,
which were watering. Remember?
You couldn't see and almost
lost your ground when you tried to stand.
So weak you have always been,
so simple and strange.

Poem for My First Girlfriend

Jessie fell through me
like wind slipping through a screen,
the way hands push through water.
For sixteen years before we met,
I never knew the feel of my own body,
how I might look at myself
if I had entertained the possibility
of not lying beneath
but lying with, one sound—
no ocean for the shell to hold.

Poem for My First Girlfriend

"I've waited my whole life for you," I thought,
as she carved *Jessie Loves Steven*
into her notebook cover so no one would know
she meant me. Back then, we still
put our cigarettes out in the cups of warm soda
at the bedside. Back then, our bodies
were rendered speechless.

I don't remember when it was I realized
the laws of flesh were the same
as the laws of creation only
we rise out of our own rib cages.

But you never cared about real origins, writing
my fake name over and over, breathing in the scent
of our bodies absorbed in your pillowcase.

"Tell me everything," you'd say, naked and smiling.
And again I would tell you, "I already did."

Prince, the Androgynous

When I listen to Prince, I feel bad about calling him a sissy.
When I listen to Prince, it's impossible to think of anything
but Prince. He's not the kind of person you can ignore.
He *just wants your extra time.* He just wants you to *act your age,*
mama, not your shoe size. And you can't say the guy doesn't
have a recipe for relationship success. Prince, the wise. Prince,
the androgynous. Prince, the scarved beauty. Prince, the revolution.
Prince, the purple rain. Prince, the computer blue. Prince, the homophobe.
Prince, the God. Prince, the Jehovah's Witness. Prince, the Seventh
Day Adventist. Prince, the little-man syndrome. Prince, the sage.
Prince, the guitar riff. Prince, the boy-girl. Prince, the prince of pop.

I tried on his moves at Wednesday night bowling alley karaoke.
He would have been appalled, really—at my mullet, at my
flippant attitude toward whether or not I could really sing,
at how I made "Little Red Corvette" sound like a prepubescent
country song, at my being in a bowling alley in the first place.
Those were the days when people smoked in bowling alleys,
the days when bowling alleys were not for families, the days
when bowling alleys were full of idle men. They thought of me
as one of them, cheered me on as I leaned
into the mic—no prince, no royalty in sight.

If I Were a Man, She'd Be in Love with Me

This is what Samantha says
from underneath the thin sheets
at the Midway Motel, where
we can rent the rooms by the hour
and the manager doesn't ask for ID.

By now I am used to high school girls
who wish I could become their prince,
their mother's favorite, their well-dressed
prom date. But instead I'm trapped
in the constellation of my nipples
and the silver moon of my belt buckle.
They try not to think of me naked,
only of themselves and of my tongue
tracing the curves in their breasts.

Driving home, she doesn't let me
rest my hand on her thigh.
We are hiding from the eyes
of passing cars like first-time adulterers.
If I were a man, I'd kiss her hard
at traffic lights, I'd wait at her locker
with the other boyfriends, I'd never
leave her in the ruin of one short
teenage orgasm. She'd be in love
with me. She really would.

On the Occasion of Being Mistaken for a Man by the Cashier in the
Drive-Thru Window at a Wendy's in Madison, Wisconsin

When a woman does it, I feel more like a man.
Simone at the Wendy's drive-thru makes me feel
more like a man when she says, "Out of ten, Sir?"
and leans her breasts atop the little shelf, smiles
at the folding windows. "You have gorgeous hands,"
I say. I can't even see her hands, but tonight
I have license to compliment, to tell Simone
I have never seen more delicate hands.

In a perfect world, I wouldn't tell Simone I was
an "anatomical female" until our fourth date.
I would include this in the same sentence I tell her
my grandparents speak Slovak and my brother
is a restaurant owner. And Simone would sway in
and kiss my neck and say, "Isn't that interesting?"
Over dinner with her parents, her father would
not forget to ask me about my brother, about
whether we could all go out for a free meal.

In a perfect world, Simone's voice is a cocoon,
an agent of transformation, and Simone is a
drive-thru queen who gives us all permission
to stop dividing like cells, to stop her from leaving me
on our fourth date and never speak a word about me.

Coming Out in Porch Light

When I tell my mother I am in love
with a woman, the kitchen turns
into a waiting room, and she opens
the newspaper to learn a local man
has committed suicide—the refrigerator
hums. She doesn't speak or cry.
I do not look at her. In this family,
we pretend not to notice change
in the eyes, or a warm rush
of feeling in the face. I focus on the window,
on the neighbor who turns on her porch light,
shaking out her quilt on the railing,
settling into a lawn chair—the quilt
draped over her lap, her thin ankles.

My mother gives up reading.
She moves the silverware
from sink to dishwasher,
first knives, then spoons, then staring
at the sponge floating in the sauce pan.
She says how late it's getting, how tired
she has been. She turns the lock
on the front door, the sound of her steps
heavy to her room where she does not sleep,
her mind flush full with pastors
who pray hate for the damned,
who hold protest signs at funerals.
She thinks of men who shove bodies
against walls at gas stations. She hears
slurs shouted from car windows.
She thinks of men who breathe
intimidation, men like my father,
by now, long gone. She imagines
a busted lip on my boyish face.

Through the window, I watch the neighbor
folding up the quilt in the porch light.
For a moment, I think she is my mother,
folding up my life into equal parts.
I fold the newspaper—on one side,
there was no note. On the other,
survived by his family.

On the Occasion of Being Mistaken for a Man by a Waiter
While Having Breakfast with My Mother

Let's just cut right to the chase. The waiter says,
"You and your son have exactly the same smile."
My mother starts scraping the black burnt off her toast
and the dark chips are falling in her butter
like dead ants. And I can't drink my juice,
which doesn't really seem like juice anymore.

I just want to go back to before,
before tomboy turned into butch,
before my father's will pulled me down from treetops,
before I started making Barbie kiss the Cabbage Patch doll named Lena,
before baseball and the movie *Dirty Dancing*
(because don't we all want to be Patrick Swayze?)
before collecting frogs and running from the kissing girls on the playground
(you know those girls who run around and kiss the boys? well, they kissed me, too)
before I stopped being escorted to public bathrooms by my mother,
before high school cheerleaders who were "just experimenting,"
before giving a blow job, before giving another blow job,
before this breakfast with my mother in which she is chewing
her eggs like they are lint from the screen in our dryer, which is always broken.
I just want to go back to before, but I am not before.

I am *after,* after fourteen lovers and trying to stop counting,
after thirteen have left me for other women,
after three black leather jackets and no bike,
after three phases of lesbian haircuts,
after realizing I am now afraid to climb trees,
after five brands of lesbian chic cigarettes,
after loving straight women like Sappho poems,

after therapy,
after touching the first breast that was not mine,
after hanging out at sports bars because in the eighties it was the only place
to find a dyke who was really serious about being a dyke,
after reading *Leaves of Grass*,
after hanging my hat on bedposts,
after all, *after* is all about posts,
I am after, I am post, post-feminist,
post-structuralist, postpartum, post-lesbian,
post-gender, I am the un-gender, post-capitalist,
post...office, but I am not sending away for anything,
not mailing anything out. I am *after* that.
I am post. I am posting up a sign and it says,
"Stand back," cause not every move I make
is the move of a woman, says the waiter.
I am after, I am after my mother who is still before.
I am after the stupid ice bobbing up and down in her drink,
so stupid it doesn't even know it is always already
made out of wet. It is always before, as I am before,
before gender, before poetry, before my rattling knees,
before you—I am before you.

On the Occasion of Being Mistaken for a Man by Security Personnel at Newark International Airport

It's like being born again, these metal detectors
are like traveling through the womb, the buzz
goes off to indicate the birth of trouble.
And the gender of trouble matters because
when a woman goes through, Jimmy yells,
"Female Search" and a large woman appears
from behind her security table. So when I walk through
and my wallet chain sets off the womb alert,
I wait. I wait for "Female Search" like I wait for the bus,
that hopeful and expectant look. But Jimmy takes me
himself. Jimmy slides his hands down the length
of my thighs. He pats his palm stiffly against my crotch.
He asks me to remove my boots and jacket,
and so I do. And at first, the woman in me goes unnoticed.
But when I hold my arms straight out
and he traces the outline of my underarms, he makes
that face, the face I've seen before,
the "holy-shit-it's-a-woman" face,
the "pretend-you-don't-notice-the-tits" face.

Jimmy's hands change from a tender sweep
to a kind of wiping, like he's trying to rid my body
of the afterbirth. He is preparing to peel off the skin of my body
as he would the apple he brings to work for break time.

Jimmy stares hard at the metal detector
with a kind of respect, like the arc of it became holy,
transformed me on my walk through.
Jimmy is nervous for the following reasons:

He has just felt the crotch and chest of a woman he thought was a man.
He cannot decide which way he liked her best.
His supervisor might notice he has not yelled "Female Search,"
which he knows is grounds for some sort of lawsuit.
He's angry, his blue uniform makes him angry,

so that when he is patting her down now, he does it with force.
He wants her to feel he is stronger than she is,
he wants the metal detector to stop being a gender-change machine
from which this woman, who is also me, emerges,
unties her boots slowly, follows all his directions.
And when Jimmy is done, he nods. He wants me
to keep him secret, to pretend neither of us had ever been born.

What It Means to Inherit

The part of me who is my father
does not weep.

I dreamt that after dinner
I realized I had swallowed
my father's heart.

I catch myself looking at women
the way he did. I catch myself
lingering in the trance of hips
and thinking they are for me.

Before sleep, like my father,
I pull sadness into my bedroom
the way the butcher pulls in his awning
at closing time.

The June night my father died
I could see my own breath.

I am in the Ladies Room.
I am wetting my hair.
When I look at my reflection,
it is my father wetting his hair.
We are both in the wrong place.

Whatever longing I have,
I never call it that.

What the Fire Teaches

I was not allowed to throw logs
on the fire, or to prod and shift
the logs already ablaze. My father
made us sit five feet away, the screen
between us, its chorus of breath and snap,
its blue-orange muttering. I squinted
to bring the flames closer. I knew
that it was terribly hot, that it could
become aggressive and uncontained.
It could destroy the house
before I could save the catfish.
I didn't know, I couldn't imagine,
why my father needed to keep us away.
He needed to be the only one
who could move each log in flame.
And now as I learn
to move like that kind of man,
I set the fire. I move each log.
I startle and panic
when the fragile get too close.

Dear Gender

When you cry, the moon doesn't stand a chance.
Our faith in you—we don't lose enough sleep
over it. Regret leans against the jukebox as if to say,
"Tell me about it." So you roll up your sleeves,
dip your hands into the deep blue of another's thighs.
You tread water until the shoreline is speculation.

And when I say, "Gender, you're going to be all right,"
what I mean is the heart is the most overworked muscle
in the body, that you won't drown out there. Forgive
yourself. Write your name in water. I will make you
into God. I will let you answer prayers at last.

Choke

To think of giving birth as a power
is to think of being a woman, I suppose,
which is to think of being whole when

I am only a fragment. Sounding off
the echoes of my own making,
I, too, am a kind of mother.

I keep giving birth to identity.
And each time it holds me
by the throat until I say words.

My mother sings, folding laundry
in the basement, under a single hanging bulb,
a spotlight for the motion of her hands

which fill the air, like conductor hands,
raised over the stale water of the floor drain,
elegant even in the lint and dust.

If Adam came from dust, I imagine it
hanging on the light bulb above my mother,
waiting to name "spider" behind the water heater,

waiting to name "woman" under the light.
Dust is watching her set socks atop the dryer.
The morning waits outside the window.

Last night I dreamt a madman in an airport
shot all the women waiting for a flight to Santa Fe.
He lined me up with the men, and I lived.

The body has its invariably public dimension: constituted as a social phenomenon in the public sphere, the body is and is not mine. Given over from the start to the world of others, bearing their imprint, formed within the crucible of social life, the body is only later, and with some uncertainty, that to which I lay claim as my own.

Judith Butler

b

e myself there,
e chromosomes
nds
t don't scar—
outs out
lms.

efore
led out

.

Dear Gender

The river holds its breath, wanting badly
to be heard, but too still for sound.

There are rooms I've loved you in.

I've never been much good at mornings.
It's the newness that bothers me.

I am told I like folk songs,
and women with long hands.

So I strap the past to my back,
I take the maps, the dry bread.

I've left you this poem at the door.

To a Woman Who Has Never Been My Lover

What I have left of this town is January,
its mouth open. I return as a fugitive,
a rusted pipeline to my past. I hoped,
didn't I, that the cloud above the trestle
would have lifted by now, or dripped
its body into the river? I had hoped
suffering had given up on being a rooftop,
and the possibilities had all put parentheses
around their names. Assume I am laboring
to say this, assume the streetlights are out again.
Assume there is a man under my skin.

I do wish we had a ceiling fan above the bed.
I keep thinking I could put one in.

There are no more ways to write to you
without announcing all I have become,
and there is no way to announce these things
without reminding you we were always strangers.
It turns out, I'm not what you thought.
It turns out, my body is refurbished
and made of ill-fitting scraps.

I've taken to long walks in the city.
I lay out my clothes in the evenings.

I am still my father's disciple, I am still
made up of long lists. If we had a chance
to talk, we might decide to bury the highway,
to make certain I don't return, at least
not now, not when we've come this close,
the river leading us out.

XY

The doctor, who speaks slowly, after spending quite a few moments
by himself in his gray office, says there is a strong possibility I am
"chromosomally mismatched," which cannot be determined now unless
I pay for the test. But the test is not necessary due to the fact that I am
"out of the danger zone." The danger zone is puberty, he says, when
"women like me" are at risk for developing genital abnormalities. I
think back to myself at thirteen, staring at my body. And I think it might
have made sense to me somehow, if my clitoris had grown like a wild
flower and hung its petals between my thighs, which were plumping up
in that adult woman way. The doctor is careful with me, knowing how
my being XY makes me a bad example of a woman: an XY woman is an
ex-woman, whose blood has been infected by Y—the testosterone an
uprising, a fire in her blood.

The doctor looks mostly at his chart. He wants me to disappear, to
put back in order his faith in the system of things. He wants me to
react correctly, to be ashamed. I sit nervously in the paper robe, which
covers only the front of my naked body. The cold laboratory air drifts
up through the gown. My nipples harden like the heads of screws.
He doesn't know he's given me a second chance at my body: I think
about the man I could have been. I make a list of names and settle on
"Michael," after my father, who did not love me. I imagine the girls in
high school I would have been able to love. Michael could have saved
me from all of this, from the sound of my voice, from the years of
wearing that church dress, which was someone else's skin. Michael is
the easier version of me. When the doctor leaves, I shove his crumpled
paper gown in the crotch of my briefs. I cover my chest with the eye
chart and try to look for Michael. But he is not able to be seen. He
is out emptying the trash at the curb. He is in me in that way a man
is in a woman.

Love Poem to Androgyny

I don't know why I love you.
I don't know why you leave me

whenever I am faced with my own body.
In my loose clothes and walk, you say
"secret" and "muscle." Outside the dumpsters
are lifted and emptied. I slide the white shirt

over my head. Last night I had
the coward dream again, the airport,
Santa Fe, gunshots echo off
the women's bodies. I stand
in the line of men and watch.

We all love you to begin with.
Then something happens. We become
a mother who races down the steps
to cover our daughter (who is riding her bike

topless) with a plaid blanket. All these years
you have been my skin though I am afraid
to say sometimes I don't love you at all.
Sometimes, it is a man I love.

In the beginning was the word, and the word
knows us. We don't always return the favor.

Fixing My Voice

When Dr. Reardon says he can "fix my voice,"
he means he will give me shots of estrogen,
which will surge through my body like electric shocks
and send the hair on my chin and stomach running
for cover. He doesn't want me to be warm.

He doesn't want to listen to my large truck voice
fill his office like the soy milk bursting up
from the bottom of his morning coffee.
He wants me to be an affirmation.

He wants me perched on his plastic table
with smooth naked legs, singing hymns
in the voice of a woman who needs him
in order to recover some piece of herself

that has been swallowed by the jaws of testosterone,
opening and closing hard like the doors of angry lovers.
He doesn't exactly know that he hates me—
the feeling is more like gender indigestion,

how the sound of my voice keeps rising
up in his throat. And he can't rid himself
of the image of my lover, who stretches out
nude in our bed and presses her hand
to my chest saying,

"talk to me, please, talk."

To a Woman Who Has Never Been My Lover

Pittsburgh is as much like an envelope
as it is like an island between rivers.
I miss you. I haven't written much of anything
but a few bad love poems and letters
I send to Long Island just for show.

It is Saturday and it is raining.
I have been thinking of learning
to speak Slovak or to play guitar.

I live above a drugstore now.
We don't have wood floors anymore.
I am still making love to the same woman.
I have finally learned that she is not a poem.

The squirrels are just as afraid, the raindrops
just as much like diamonds.

I am writing to tell you
I have lost my favorite notebook
and the museums all look at me
like they're dying. I don't think
I am a woman anymore. I don't like
potlucks or bars or my breasts.

How are you? Does the chapel
still look that way, like it will
slip down the hill and block the road?

At a Rest Stop in Central Pennsylvania, a Man Chokes Me for Talking to His Girlfriend But, Thankfully, Lets Me Go After Referring to Me as a "Man-Dyke Freak of Nature"

When he first grabs me, I'm leaving the women's room.
His knuckles are locked like fat bolts beneath my chin.
My pulse buzzes beneath skin like an old radiator.

My breasts want to sink into my sweat-covered chest,
to become hollow burrows like the ones small animals
dig into soft enough, wet enough landscape.

And when he loosens his grip, my head is the roof
of a burning house. A woman turns her gas cap. It clicks.
This is how we know when we've gone far enough.

Of course, there is never anything else to do but leave.
My car, a burglarized residence. I turn the mirrors
face up. I have no wish to see myself, traveling or not.

These days I fuel up before leaving. I piss on the shoulders
of highways, even on the cold and black nights when urine
spreads out around my shoes like a high tide around rocks,

the warm steam rising as if it were fog off the river bank,
the yellow haze of it sucked in by the yellow moon.
Sometimes, I can smell it in the floor mats all the way home.

Reading *Stone Butch Blues*
for Leslie Feinberg

When the men rape you in the schoolyard,
I open my high school yearbook and
cut out the faces of girls I wanted to love.
I let the sink run for hours, tip over
the bookcases, melt away the candles
in defiance of lovers who insist
on lighting up the body.

When drag queens take you in like their first-born son,
I go out into the autumn air and rake the dying
leaves from the grass. I fill black trash bags,
pretend I don't live here when the postman comes.
When you land your first job at a factory,
tuck your breasts away like laundered money,
I polish all the tables, call my mother.

When they break your jaw, my voice explodes
into stars, my hands become honeycombs
and my mouth an untrained soldier.
But the stars I make freeze up, and all I can do
is thank you, Sweet Father, for my life.

Talk Show

The audience is heckling and laughing.
Billie Jo sits with her legs spread
like garden shears, explains a lesbian stud
is *solely a pleasure-giver.* And after the
"I-wish-my-man-would-take-lessons-from-you"
and the "I-need-to-lose-my-zero-because-
you're-my-hero" bullshit, this happens:

They all want to know, even Ricki,
why Billie Jo looks like a man. After all
she is such a pretty girl, one woman says.
"You're making us look bad,"
some husband complains. Distribution
of pleasure is such a tricky business.
And I'm not sure I trust Billie Jo.

Weeks later I'm leaving the Taco Bell,
and after the cashier stumbles through
the space between "sir" and "miss,"
two men prowl behind me saying,
"Let's follow it home and find out."

And I'm not sure I trust Billie Jo,
even when my lover eases her hand
inside me and my body is a slip-knot,
a ticking pocket watch. I grip her forearm
with my fingernails, scrape them
down to her thin wrist.
I can't, I say, *I just can't.*

Penis Envy

They know I am not one of them,
the women in single-file lines
who grip purses, pulling close
to the body what matters most.

I am a thief of spaces. They check
the signs on the door. They match
their reactions to the other women
around them. One woman, certain:
my eyelashes are a dead giveaway.

From Laramie

I can't look
at the fences.
My body
takes a leave
of absence
before turning
into wildfire.
Signs litter
the open road.
The wind
has the trees
in a holdup
until they
let go
of the rain,
which slips
through
the branches
with such
simple rage.

For Tomboys

When the neighborhood kids realize you are not a boy,
run—head-tucked, arm-pumping, leg-burning run.

Don't hang around the soccer field to see what they might do.
Don't wait for any of them to press your body against a tree

while the others pull down your pants. Don't wait for reactions,
hoping they still choose you as team captain, still share their water.

Don't freeze up. Don't urinate in fear or shame. Try to forget
scoring your third goal of the afternoon. Forget Shannon Wallace

smiling in your direction, how the boys on your team high-fived,
forget that your hands and their hands smacked with sweat

like a kind of boy religion, that the soccer field was boy church,
until the neighborhood kids realize you are not a boy. Run.

Run hard. Run through the bushes—no matter how thick or thorned,
run like you're chasing down the offense, run away from the gold chain

dangling from Vinny Aiello's neck, the crucifix reflecting
the relentless sun. Run from the burning field, run away

from them circling you in the wooded pines, their fingers arrows
in your pounding chest. Run now. For your life. Run.

A Poem in Response to Those Who Argue That My Desire to Purposefully Remove My Breasts is an Anti-Feminist Notion

Keep in mind I weigh a buck eighty-five
and this is not about a desire for less flesh.
Keep in mind that celebrating womanhood is a trap
and that the men's shirts I like to wear
are not conducive to a breast environment.

Admit that it's your body you want me to celebrate,
that you want my assurance that your own breasts
are a part of your picture ID card for the woman club.

What a paradise it would be to think not in halves, but tops and bottoms.
I'm all man on the top and woman on the bottom.
See how that works, all man on the top and woman on the bottom?

You may be wondering about my mind. After all,
we wouldn't want mind to be man, and it happens to be on top.
Mind on top, woman on the bottom.
See how that works?
Mind on top, and woman on the bottom.

But my mind is not a man. In fact, my mind
hates my man because my man is always trying to be on top,
and mind is on top, mind has to be on top.

You still want to me to say what I would call myself then,
being all man on the top and woman on the bottom?
You still want me to name it, to name
what my vagina and breast-less chest
would mean or be called? I say, *You do it*.
It is you who have been naming me all along.

On the Occasion of Being Mistaken for a Man by a Pregnant Woman to Whom I Have Relinquished My Bus Seat

She is "glad to know there are still gentlemen
lingering in the city." And I am suddenly proud.
I am one of those men who opens car doors,
who pays for dinner and expects nothing in return.
But even the kind of man I am has secrets.

The bus jerks away from a traffic light.
We all tip a little forward then back.
I watch her breasts dip down and
touch the top of her round belly.

I did want her seat, but the eyes of two elderly men
and a woman with a violin singled me out
as the one gentleman who would rise
and gesture toward his blue seat.

But I am not having the thoughts of a gentleman.
I imagine her water breaks. I imagine a cloudy fluid
flowing into a small river at my feet in the aisle,
my sneakers wet with the preface to birth.

Maybe I'd like to be a mother, to be the pregnant woman
to whom some gentleman relinquishes his bus seat,
the swollen flesh of my breasts bobbing, foreign.

Maybe, in some other world, I won't be standing,
holding tight to this bar for balance. I won't feel
like I owe anybody anything. My water will break
on a bus, and my body will have learned to speak for itself.

Dear Gender

Leave me here. Take your scarred
hands away from my hairline, sweat
dripping like water over stone.

You grab me like a lover,
tender and forceful. You make me
dust collecting on a violin

the owner hasn't played since
he dreamt he was the ocean.
Gender, you are not a moon hung

over Pittsburgh. You take what you can get
and send my silence cross-country—
no money for tolls, no phone numbers

from old lovers, no maps to live by.
You swing your legs over my hip bones.
You make me your saddle, cold leather

clinging to the back of this animal.
Gender, I want you to turn me to chain.
I want to bleed you out without dying.

IV

The androgynous mind is resonant and porous;
it transmits emotion without impediment; it is
naturally creative, incandescent and undivided.

Virginia Woolf

VI

Butch Defines Feminism under the Following Conditions

I think I have been smearing the theory
all over my wounds like an ointment,
trying to heal disappointment with all these appointments
with a therapist named Jane, whose thighs make me
dream of being Tarzan as she explains how I might
more fully appreciate my womanly body as wonderful.

And what's so wonderful about equal anyway, or
so equal about wonderful? And moreover,
men are not wonderfully equal nor are they equally
wonderful as I am full, full of sand, full of gender-contraband,
full of what I am, which is, I admit, part man if you
want to look at it that way, which is the only way you can.

Four days a week I am full of manliness.
Four days a month I am full of uncleanliness.
I am full of feminism of the stomach, of the lungs,
but a fungus is growing in my gut and looks like
a man, although it looks like me, who is a woman,

if you want to look at it that way, which is the only way you can.
Don't tell anyone I said this, but sometimes in the mirror
even feminism looks like a man. And one day a week
I want to grow a great big penis and walk around
saying things like "hey, suck my dick." But I know
my lover wouldn't like that. She is a feminist like me.

Don't get me wrong, feminism is not actually a man,
just looks like one in the mirror, and the definition is getting clearer
because I have to end up the hero of this poem, or the heroine,
if you want to look at it that way, which is the only way you can.
I've got feminism between my legs
and she is as fierce and tender as a lover.
I've got feminism, but feminism keeps
turning me over on my back in the bathtub,

has me pinned, has me woman-ed.
And this is where the definition begins:
there has to be something in there about rights and dykes,
something in there about eating meat, about dating cheats,
about calling them tits, about getting hit, about the rules
and tools of the patriarch because we hate that arch,
the one above us, as arches usually are, as we walk
through and under, through and under.

Changing the Names

In the eighth grade, I told a girl
my name was Ben. I kissed her with my
mouth in that eighth-grader-in-love
sort of way. It wasn't the name she loved.

In Pittsburgh, the rivers want to freeze over,
but can't stay still long enough. So, for a while,
I call them ice to honor their wanting,
their leaving and returning, always the
slow shift of hands and water.

The Clownfish

How they change is a mystery,
and takes only a few hours,
shimmering with color against
the backdrop of the coral reef,
hiding in crevices for safety.
Sometimes from male to female,
sometimes female to male,
sometimes spending their clown-
fish lives as neither gender,
sometimes as hybrid, as both.

The scientists call it "sexual
plasticity." The scientists say
the clownfish and their ray-finned
friends change their genders
to *maximize fertility.* But
fuck the scientists. They're clown-
fish after all, making gender
into their honking rubber noses.
Perhaps their genders are a thousand
clowns emptying out of a clown car.
Perhaps it's all for a great laugh,
or a great grief, or a great love.

But make no mistake, the scientists
would like to stop them. One fish-
gender specialist in New Hampshire
has been trying for years to stop
the black sea bass from going
through their FTM sex changes.
He wants "more successful breeding."
But the fish won't quit. And "it just gets
worse in captivity," he says, leaning
against the tank in his lab coat.

It's clear he's grown fond of them,
the sea bass pressing their spongy
bodies against the glass, pushing at
the boundary between the water
and the threat of the open air.

The Kind of Man I Am at the DMV

Mommy, that man is a girl, says the boy
pointing his finger, like a narrow spotlight,
targeting the center of my back, his kid-hand
learning to assert what he sees, his kid-hand
learning the failure of gender's tidy little story
about itself. I try not to look at him

because, yes, that man is a girl. I, man, am a girl.
I am the kind of man who is a girl, and because
the kind of man I am is patient with children,
I try not to hear the meanness in his voice,
his boy-voice that sounds like a girl-voice
because his boy-voice is young and pitched high
like the tent in his pants will be years later
because he will grow to be the kind of man
who is a man, or so his mother thinks.

His mother snatches his finger from the air.
Of course he's not, she says, pulling him back
to his seat. *What number does it say we are?*
she says to her boy, bringing his attention
to numbers, to counting and its solid sense.

But he has earrings, the boy complains,
now sounding desperate, like he's been
the boy who cried wolf, like he's been
the hub of disbelief before. But this time
he knows he is oh-so-right. The kind
of man I am is a girl, the kind of man
I am is pushups-on-the-basement-floor,
is chest-bound-tight-against-himself,
is thick-gripping-hands-to-the-wheel
when the kind of man I am drives away
from the boy who will become a boy,

except for now, while he's still a girl-voice,
a girl-face, a hairless arm, a powerless hand.
That boy is a girl, that man who is a girl
thinks to himself as he pulls out of the lot,
his girl eyes shining in the Midwest sun.

Explication: Intersexual

Take, for instance, my body,
always the flag at half-mast,
or carving initials,
the wind's leave of absence,
someone saying *what are you,*
photographs and their edges.

Take washing the wine glass
of a man who once rocked himself
calm inside your lover's body.

Take the water tower in a town
where rows of pawnshops
dip into the sidewalks
with their old cameras
and bicycles.

Take dressing a wound,
dropping anchor, the long
stare of strangers from train
windows marked by palms.

Take, carefully, this mouth—
its house tongue full
of brush fire and pine.

Biographies of Hands

I'm up writing biographies
of hands. I remember folding
the blanket, scraping ash.

I'm up with the matchbook,
with the crickets' silver sound.
I'm up with the thought of you,
my body still making the wrong offer,

the planes overhead, the possible
deaths of houseplants.
I used to say I'm refusing
to rest though tonight mostly

I'm wanting something
more specific
like the window screen
like your voice
like transformation
like more masculine hands.

What is safe haven
for words or for body.

Sandhill Crane Information Session

for Jan Beatty

Dan says the cranes are monogamous for life,
been that way for 10,000 years—unless
there's no baby. "They keep at it," he jokes,
"but if there's no offspring, they split."
Jan and I sit queer in the rows of khaki shorts,
among reproductive citizens with cameras.
Jan is protected, no matter how warm the air,
in the cool wrap of her black Harley jacket,
making wisecracks in my ear. Her smooth
radio voice: *Hey, man, what's with this guy?*
We can barely breathe, and all we wanted
was the Platte River and the cranes returning
to the water. We can feel we don't belong here
with Dan, we don't belong here with the kids
tugging at purses, tying their shoes together.

Why can't we come up with better reasons
to fuck one another, better reasons for why
the cranes decide to call it quits? And besides,
it's not that interesting to talk about *not* fucking.
And no matter how many cranes stop fucking
the same crane, no matter how many baby cranes
are born or not born, no matter how many children
ignore Dan's slide show, no matter how many times
someone lies about what's natural or evolutionary,
no matter how many rings we put on our fingers,
no matter how much we want, no matter how still
or how freezing the river gets, the Sandhill Cranes,
they stay alive. They sing all night.

Conversation with My Student, James

"How did you like this book, James?"

"This book is so gay," James says.

"Do you mean to say the book is happy, or homosexual?"

"I mean gay like stupid gay."

"James, how would you like it if every time I thought something
was stupid I said, *That's so James*?"

"That's different," he says. "James is a real name."

Letter from Thomas Beattie to the Media

after Bassey Ikpi

This is me, pregnant, all man-chest
and man-chin, resting above a protruding
man-belly, bursting with the burden of baby birth.

This is me, pregnant, feet strapped up
in stirrups at the obstetrician, my legs
unshaven, my gender a *both-at-once*
in the face of fragile certainty.

There was a time you did not know me,
a time your safe sense of this or that
held you at night like an old blanket.
I do realize I've broken you.
I do realize I've sent you into a frenzy.

But this is me, pregnant, carrying a new life
in my man-body, pushing a baby through my
man-vagina, which I kept for such an occasion,
its hair coarse and thick with testosterone surge.

And you loathe me, even Oprah shifts in her chair:

>   *But how could you ...*
>   *But how will you ...*
>   *But won't it be ...*

This is me, pregnant, and there you are
with your God made this
and your God made that.

What you really know when you see me
is that God made a pregnant man. You know
God made gender a plaything. God made

gender a tire swing, some monkey bars.
God made gender an infinite playground.

This is me, pregnant, and I just might give birth
to a whole world, a whole nation of gender-fuckers
rising out from my inevitable and impossible womb.

Dear Gender

It was like this when I saw
the owl lift from the throat
of a tree, the leaves scraping
the thin spine of branches.

Sometimes there's no excuse:
the cawings of yellow birds.
We had taken rainstorms into
ourselves. Our chests
lock up as vaults.
We slice through the vines
of noon. We're hoping
nets unfold beneath
whatever is falling away,
whatever grief you are,
whatever plunges, rings.

Elegy

Tonight I died my father's death
and the crows were perched
outside the pale green walls,
still (at first) as soldiers.

They are nothing like
my grandfather's pigeons
that lifted from his hands
as I watched them turn
to splinters in the gray sky.

For my father, death smelled
like a woman's hair
hanging over him,
brushing his face.
The crows lift off the power lines.
This is the place we all go. My father
presses his hands against his chest
with no authority. His body
will open up, bloom almost,
slow, like a sunrise.

His eyes float out of hospital windows,
and outside the crows are singing,
and their wings are unfolding,
fluttering long like the pages
of a thousand books, as though
there were something to leave behind.

Gendered Offerings

Your fingers moments
before the gesture. The house
and its rosebush. Look at me,
only approximation, the delicate
slip. All day I take care.
All day along the rib.
The bed being made,
a hole dug in the yard
tracing the pipe to water.
Your father sings bluegrass.
My charcoal clothes,
what binds my chest
at the closet floor.
The stretch of sky above
the city, which waits
so humbly for its rain.
I carry this to our bed,
where each night the body
loses its memory, and
for a moment, is able to give.

On the Occasion of Being Mistaken for a Woman by a Therapist in the South Hills of Pittsburgh

Tell me again, she says, *how you liked being Hansel*
in the sixth grade production of Hansel and Gretel.
She leans in close. *You've told me how it feels*
to be a man, how about how it feels to be a woman?

And I remember how it felt to play the woodcutter's son:
the tight grip of the suspenders on my shoulders,
Lila Henning's small hands as she played the role
of my sister, how she pushed Mrs. Gladys,
who played the conspiring candy-house witch,
into the oven. I was a good Hansel. I practiced
making the disappointed face for the moment
we realize the birds have eaten the breadcrumb trail.

It feels wrong to be a woman, wrong when
the barista at the café says *have a nice day*
ladies, wrong when my mother calls
my underwear *panties,* wrong when
my hair is tied in pigtails. I do not speak
the language of women, and the therapist
is trying to unwind me. She thinks, of course,
that I must know what it is like, that
somewhere deep inside me lives the life
of a woman, if I would only let her speak.

I sit still. I sit like Hansel locked in his cage.
The witch, after all, plans on eating him.
If I thought a woman were there, I would go
look for her. I am the kind of man who rescues,
who thinks to leave a failing trail in the forest.
I am the woodcutter's son, unwanted,
but finally, after a close call with death,
held closely and welcomed home.

My Mother's Hands

Once they belonged to the nuns, once
her left was slapped with a switch, once
her left hand was the devil's hand, the same
hand she used when the nuns made her touch
the dead body of a dead nun she did not
know at the Catholic open casket funeral.

Once they scanned groceries at the A&P,
once they held the burden of her father's war,
once they held the fragile tilt of infants,
once earth in my mother's hands, once
black tea, once my teenage tears, once
her mother's impenetrable "no," once
in my mother's hands, nails bitten down,
once this China cabinet cut, once this
island, once this town, once this ricochet
of sound, this symphony of survival.

As a Woman Sometimes Does to a Man

Blind fog rising off
the lit city, your body

again against the white sheets.
Your body is not your mother's

prayer. And when, in winter,
the river freezes over

and the church bells
go unnoticed into our chests,

is it enough to say
I want to see you

brush lint from my jacket,
straighten my collar,

as a woman sometimes
does to a man she takes

great care in offering to
the terrible visible world?

Unlearning the Body with My Grandfather

I dream he breathes out
candles in a dark hall
which feels like a tunnel
except for it's this house,
this hallway outside
the bedroom door.

I remember he says
what small grace
and *there are places*
you can't bring this
kind of body. There's
a pitch black
to my following him,

always the hospital robe,
always the last memory.

He wouldn't have known me
to make love to a woman,
but in the dream,
we seemed to recognize
each other with more precision,
with each lost flame.

There were times he'd lift me
up into trees. You cannot
think of any specific kind
of tree, only it mustn't
be tied to the earth.

Acknowledgements

Grateful acknowledgment is made to the journals in which some of these poems originally appeared:

Black Warrior Review: "Remembering a Full Moon, Threaded"
Bloom: "Letter from Thomas Beattie to the Media" and "On the Occasion of Being Mistaken for a Boy by the Umpire at the Little League Conference Championship"
Chiron Review: "To A Woman Who Has Never Been My Lover"
Columbia Poetry Review: "In the Second Grade Robby O'Reilly Punches Me in the Eye Because I Lost the Garter Snake I Was Supposed to Watch While He Went Camping with His Father in Maine" and "The Kind of Man I Am at the DMV"
5 AM: "XY"
Gulf Stream: "Reading *Stone Butch Blues*"
Marlboro Review: "On the Occasion of Being Mistaken for a Man by a Pregnant Woman to Whom I Have Relinquished My Bus Seat"
The Massachusetts Review: "The Monkeys"
Nimrod: "Choke" and "On the Occasion of Being Mistaken for a Man by Security Personnel at Newark International Airport"
Pearl: "Fixing My Voice"
Poet Lore: "If I Were a Man, She'd Be in Love with Me"
The Rattling Wall: "On the Occasion of Being Mistaken for a Woman by a Therapist In the South Hills of Pittsburgh" and "Tits"
West Branch: "What it Means to Inherit"
The Worcester Review: "Butch Defines Feminism under the Following Conditions"

"About Ben" appeared in *Small-Town Gay* (Kerlak Enterprises, 2004), and some of the poems from this collection also appeared in *Love Poem to Androgyny* (Main Street Rag, 2006), winner of the Main Street Rag Chapbook Competition.

I owe so much to Pittsburgh, to all the poets who sing from its bridges, and bars, and rivers, especially Ed Ochester, Lynn Emanuel, Toi Derricotte, Judith Vollmer, Jeff Oaks, Terrance Hayes, Jim Daniels, my little poet sister Kayla Sargeson, the thoughtful and handsome Tony Petrosky, and all the remarkable poets in the Madwomen in the Attic writing community. To my former and forever teachers Denise Duhamel, Saundra Morris, Patricia Terry, Joyce Sullivan, Nicole Cooley, Karl Patten, and Cynthia Hogue. Your guidance has led me always to the right places in my work and in my life. I give endless gratitude, also, to Jan Beatty with whom I would drive anywhere and who has fiercely loved these poems (and me) through many drafts and years.

I have survived some of the grief and sorrow of these poems and of gender because of the deep friendships in my life, because of those who always show up, no matter what. Thank you, Amy Schafer, Kate Benchoff, Tara Lien, Jennifer Lee, and Julie Beaulieu. I thank, always, Jessie Milana, indeed my first girlfriend, whose unmistakable laugh rings out over twenty years.

I thank my poetry brother Brandon Som for always cultivating and hearing in me the lyrical politics of identity, and Maureen Sinclair for her spiritual guidance, her faith in me always. I owe so much to my parents, Carol and Stefan Krompier, whose love for me made it possible for me to survive as myself, always. And lastly, the heart I had to offer this work was twice the heart because of the love, support, and sense of humor of Brie Owen, who makes me and my writing more clear and more alive. You are every beautiful thing I've ever wanted to say.

Other books from Tupelo Press

See our complete backlist at www.tupelopress.org